EAGLE

WORKBOOK

FOR
BECOMING THE ONE

BY
SHELEANA AIYANA

HEAL YOUR PAST, TRANSFORM YOUR RELATIONSHIP PATTERNS, AND COME TO YOURSELF.

WORKBOOK & SUMMARY

Copyright 2022 by Eagle Reads - All Rights Reserved. This summary and workbook is meant as a companion and introduction to enrich your experience of, and understanding of a formidable work of non-ficition. This workbook is by no means intended as a substitute for the work it is based upon, and it is not authorized, approved, licensed or endorsed by the work's author or publisher.

This work is geared towards providing exact and reliable information with regards to the topic covered. The publication is sold with the idea that the publisher is not required to render accounting, officially permitted or otherwise, qualified services. If advice is necessary, legal or professional, a practiced individual in the profession should be ordered. In no way is it legal to duplicate, reproduce or transmit any part of this document through either electronic means or other printed format. Any recording and storage of this work is strictly prohibited.

All Rights Reserved. Respective Authors hold all Copyrights not held by the publisher. The information contained in this work is for informational purposes only and the Publisher shall not held liable for any injury of whatever kind arising from the use of information contained in this work.

TABLE OF CONTENT

Chapter 1: The Healing Journey..............................7

Chapter 2: Is Starts With You.................................15

Chapter 3: Coming Home to the Body's Wisdom...........23

Chapter 4: Connect With Your Inner Child..................39

Chapter 5: Healing the Abandonment Wound...............47

Chapter 6: Divine Mother and Father Energy...............55

Chapter 7: Forgiveness and Acceptance.....................69

Chapter 8: Understanding Projections......................79

Chapter 9: Transform Your Relationship Patterns...........89

Chapter 10: Compassionate Self-Awareness...............97

Chapter 11: Red Flags, Green Flags........................107

Chapter 12: Trust Your Body, Set Boundaries.............113

Chapter 13: Clarify Your Expectations.....................121

Chapter 14: Define Your Core Values......................129

Chapter 15: Creating a Conscious Relationship.........137

Chapter 16: Your Path to Auhentic Love..................145

NOTE TO USERS

This is an unofficial workbook for Sheleana Aiyana's "Becoming the One" designed to enrich your experience of the original book, and give you practical steps to apply the authors' message to your life. Buy *Becoming the One* by scanning the QR code below.

A PLEA

Dear Friend,
Please, if you like this workbook, consider giving us a rating, or a review on Amazon. It will not only give the workbook more visibility, but will ultimately help more amazing people like you find it.

Cheers.

HOW TO USE THIS WORKBOOK

This workbook comprises chapter summaries of each chapter of Becoming the One, a self-reflection section based on each chapter's message, and a coloring page.

It is recommended that you first read the original work and assimilate its essence before picking up this workbook to perform the exercises. Also, references are made to the original work, so you must have it handy when working with this workbook.

Note that you do not have to perform all the exercises or answer the prompts at once; you may decide to leave out some of them and work on them at your pace.

Best wishes.

PART ONE

RECLAIM YOUR RELATIONSHIP TO SELF.

"Home is the love you have within you."

CHAPTER ONE

THE HEALING JOURNEY

When Sheleana was just three, her mother was twenty-five and a survivor of unimaginable childhood abuse, betrayal, and neglect. Because of this, she suffered from undiagnosed Complex Post-Traumatic Stress Disorder. One night, Sheleana's mom took her to a couple, left her with them, and drove away despite Sheleana's desperate cries. That particular moment was emblazoned in Sheleana and caused her to develop abandonment wounding (invisible wounds that plant deep emotional pain when not tended to properly. Symptoms include giving too much or being overly eager to please, jealousy, feeling insecure, and needing to control or be controlled). Thus, Sheleana became an adult who ignored red flags and sought love where there was none at her expense.

Unsurprisingly, by the time Sheleana was 26, she was a year into a marriage full of abuse, emotional torture, and absence of love. One day, her husband abandoned their marriage and went away with a new lover, stoking the embers of the wounds of Sheleana's history of abandonment.

Like Sheleana's story, it is common to repeatedly find yourself in the same relationship patterns. Though your relationships may seem different, emotional patterns like neediness and betrayal remain the same.

Sheleana aims to remind you and help you find the love you are with her book because your relationship with yourself is the most important relationship you will ever cultivate. Therefore, you need to come home to yourself by healing the patterns that keep you in a cycle of unhappiness and heartbreak; this is called the Healing Work.

However, you must realize that your healing path is peculiar to you, so you must never use any person or their life as a benchmark for your healing.

SELF-REFLECTION AND EXERCISES

"It is important to focus on the core emotional themes we bring into every relationship." Sheleana realized that her core emotional themes were abandonment and betrayal. Can you think of any emotional themes, positive or negative that have influenced your relationships till this moment?

_____
_____
_____
_____
_____
_____
_____
_____
_____
_____
_____
_____
_____
_____
_____
_____
_____
_____

Sheleana describes the Healing Work as grieving the past that was lost. Is there any relationship from your past that stilll hurts you? Identify and explain why it still hurts, and resolve to allow grief run its course so you can heal.

_____
_____
_____
_____
_____
_____
_____
_____
_____
_____
_____
_____
_____
_____
_____
_____
_____
_____
_____
_____
_____
_____
_____

Healing also means forgiving others and yourself. In the exercise that follows, write down who you forgive and for what. It may even be yourself.

❶

I forgive _____ for _____

_____
_____
_____
_____
_____

❷

I forgive _____ for _____

_____
_____
_____
_____
_____

❸

I forgive _____ for _____

_____
_____
_____
_____
_____

❹

*I forgive*_____ *for* _____

_____

_____

_____

_____

_____

Doing the healing work also means siting with and acknowledging big emotions that have been repressed. Do you have any emotions that you have tried to surpress all your life? Acknowledge and come face to face with them now.

_____

_____

_____

_____

_____

_____

_____

_____

_____

_____

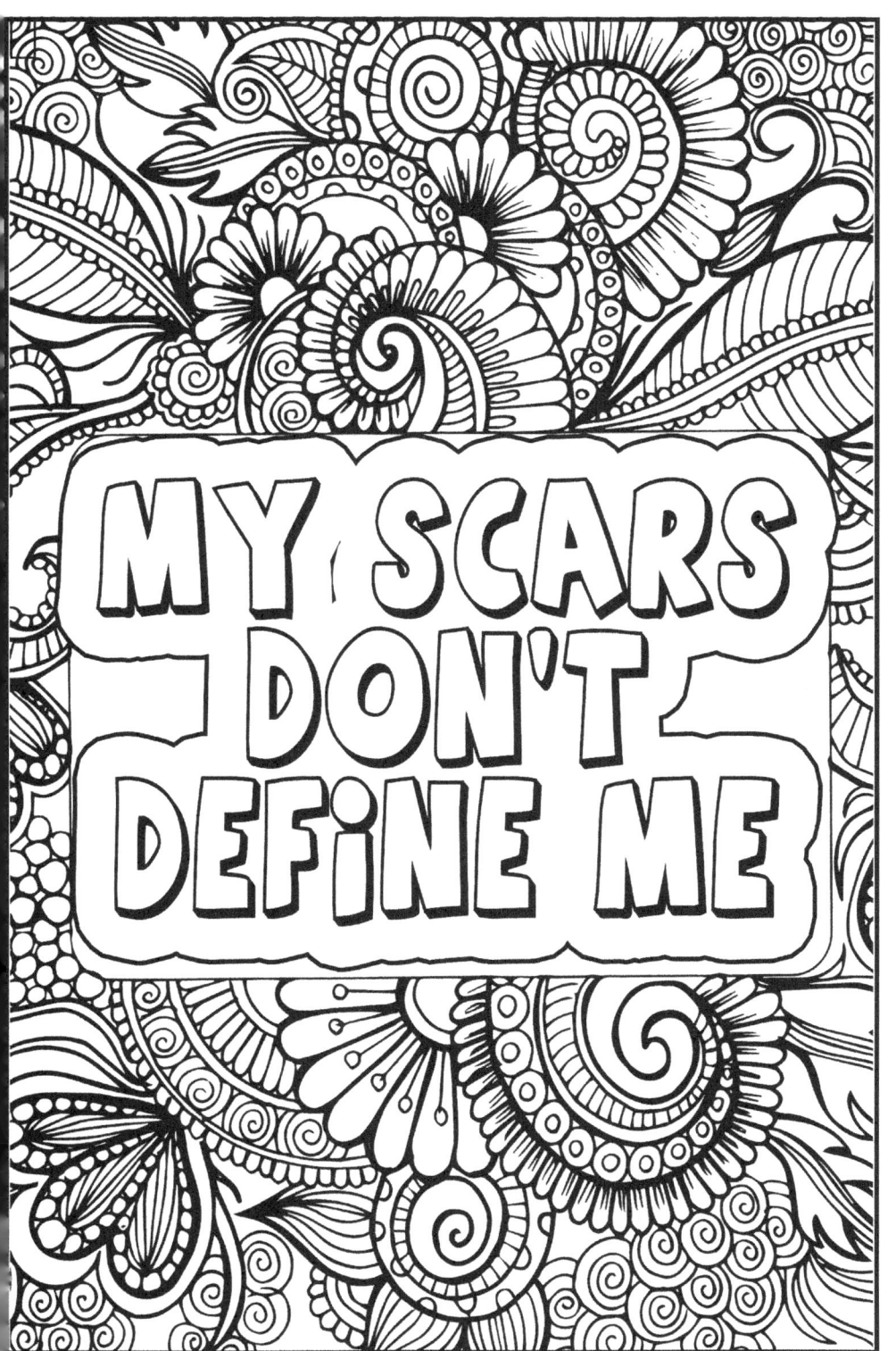

CHAPTER TWO

IT STARTS WITH YOU

Becoming One with yourself starts with you. It means doing the inner work on yourself, which must start with self-devotion. Hence, your sense of worth must not depend on something external like being in a romantic relationship, or you will permanently settle for less. Building that relationship with yourself is a gradual process of witnessing your thoughts and reconnecting to your body and the full spectrum of your emotions. It also means embracing the totality of who you are and acknowledging your power to change your situation from rejection to acceptance starting on the inside.

You must also learn to objectively assess and observe your thoughts rather than always let yourself be led by them. This is because self-observation is a crucial part of the inner work. If you don't learn to observe your mind, you end up believing every fear, every criticism, and every doubt that arises in your mind, which is terrible for your journey to a place where you are self-aware and confident. However, it's still okay if you feel disconnected from your authentic self at the moment, be patient and practice compassion for yourself by finding meaning in all your experiences.

Finally, you must know that your relationship with yourself sets the foundation for all other relationships in your life.

SELF-REFLECTION AND EXERCISES

Most times, we spend so much time and resources trying to feel better, or to not feel at all. How about being present and welcoming whatever feeling is present in you right now? Can you welcome it?

_____
_____
_____
_____
_____
_____
_____
_____
_____
_____
_____
_____

What has been the propelling factor for your relationships till this moment? Is it a desire to get the feelings you crave? Or for validation and security? If it is, acknowledge it and tell yourself you are on a journey.

_____
_____
_____
_____
_____
_____
_____
_____
_____
_____
_____
_____
_____
_____
_____
_____
_____
_____
_____
_____
_____

What has been the propelling factor for your relationships till this moment? Is it a desire to get the feelings you crave? Or for validation and security? If it is, acknowledge specific instances and tell yourself you are on a journey.

_____
_____
_____
_____
_____
_____
_____
_____
_____
_____
_____
_____
_____
_____
_____
_____
_____
_____
_____
_____

"The energy you carry matters." Do you have a feel of what your energy is like now? Describe it. It will help you realize what you need to work on.

_____
_____
_____
_____
_____
_____
_____
_____
_____
_____
_____
_____
_____
_____
_____
_____
_____
_____
_____
_____
_____
_____
_____
_____

Could you tend to all your feelings with love? Sometimes, we label our feelings and prevent ourselves from full expression. Good, bad, positive, too intense, laidback, strong, weak...which you embrace and which feelings do you deny?

_____
_____
_____
_____
_____
_____
_____
_____
_____
_____
_____
_____
_____
_____
_____
_____
_____
_____

From Sheleana's experience, people default to anger or sadness under stressful circumstances or conflict. In the exercises that follow, you will learn how to embrace your anger and sadness in an uplifting way by using your previous experiences. We shall start with anger.

CHAPTER THREE

COMING HOME TO THE BODY'S WISDOM

It is beyond debate that humans are energy-sensitive beings. Yet, this truth is what our culture has struggled to accept, prioritizing cold logic and downplaying emotionality. However, that will change for you as Sheleana will help you create a conscious relationship with your body and energetic environment after learning to observe your mind.

You must be aware that one of the major difficulties you may encounter while trying to do the inner work is how to process big emotions and sensations that you will encounter, failure to handle these emotions the right way, especially if you are not in tune with your body will lead to further disconnection and shame within you. Thus, being in and at home with your body is a key component of healing. You must realize that you don't need to ignore, justify or even fix the emotions in your body; simply learning to all discomfort run its course and letting the body move the way it wants is healing.

Being a deeply connected spiritual being means that your head, body and heart must work in glorious harmony. When you're in your head, you immediately try to rationalize and explain feelings; when you're only in your body, you notice emotions without trying to make sense of them. However, when you have a head, body and heart connection, you can differentiate between your thoughts, sensations and feelings. You trust your body and know when time and space are needed to process intense emotions while valuing emotion and logic.

Sheleana explains that our false selves have origins in our feeble attempts to survive hardship and abuse. In trying to survive, we adorn survival masks prioritizing self-preservation over building connections. Sometimes, from Sheleana's experience, people default to anger or sadness under stressful circumstances or conflict.

Finally, coming home to yourself is learning to feel safe in your body again. It is a return to the wisdom of your heart, the trust inherent in your body; a return to your intuition and worth irrespective of your relationship status, income level, external achievement or anything else.

SELF-REFLECTION AND EXERCISES

Sheleana adorned a *Survival Mask* as a shield to her vulnerability, abuse, anger and shame, by numbing her pain with drugs and alcohol, telling herself she was okay. However, acknowledging your masks can be one of the most empowering stages in your healing. In what ways are you wearing a Survival Mask?

_____
_____
_____
_____
_____
_____
_____
_____
_____
_____
_____
_____
_____
_____
_____
_____
_____
_____
_____

"Most of us know how to distract ourselves from our emotional experiences." Is this statement true for you? How can you learn to embrace your emotions through self-soothing exercises recommended by Sheleana?

From Sheleana's experience, people default to anger or sadness under stressful circumstances or conflict. In the exercises that follow, you will learn how to embrace your anger and sadness in an uplifting way by using your previous experiences. We shall start with anger.

Embracing Your Relationship to Anger

❶

Situation/Someone that makes/made me angry _____
_____
_____
_____
_____

What do I need to feel safe, respected and important? _____
_____
_____
_____
_____
_____

Do I need to remove my energy from the situations?
_____
_____
_____
_____

Do I need to take action? Why or why not? _____
_____
_____
_____

Is there another feeling besides anger that I am afraid to show?
_____
_____
_____
_____

What emotions are underneath my anger? _____
_____
_____
_____
_____

Does this situation bring up something or someone from the past?
_____
_____
_____
_____

Is it time to explore the tenderness and vulnerability under my anger?
_____
_____
_____
_____
_____

❷

Situation/Someone that makes/made me angry _____

_____
_____
_____
_____

What do I need to feel safe, respected and important? _____

_____
_____
_____
_____
_____

Do I need to remove my energy from the energy or situations?

_____
_____
_____
_____
_____

Do I need to take action? Why or why not? _____

_____
_____
_____
_____

Is there another feeling besides anger that I am afraid to show?
_____
_____
_____
_____

What emotions are underneath my anger? _____
_____
_____
_____
_____

Does this situation bring up something or someone from the past?
_____
_____
_____
_____

Is it time to explore the tenderness and vulnerability under my anger?
_____
_____
_____
_____

❸

Situation/Someone that makes/made me angry _____
_____
_____
_____
_____

What do I need to feel safe, respected and important? _____
_____
_____
_____
_____
_____

Do I need to remove my energy from the energy or situations?
_____
_____
_____
_____
_____

Do I need to take action? Why or why not? _____
_____
_____
_____

Is there another feeling besides anger that I am afraid to show?
_____
_____
_____
_____

What emotions are underneath my anger? _____
_____
_____
_____
_____

Does this situation bring up something or someone from the past?
_____
_____
_____
_____

Is it time to explore the tenderness and vulnerability under my anger?
_____
_____
_____
_____

Embracing Your Relationship to Sadness

❶

I am/was sad about _____

How can I be tender to myself in this situation _____

Where in my body do I feel sadness? _____

Is there a feeling, besides sadness that I am afraid to feel?

Would it feel good to reach out for support? If so, to who?

Is it time to shift my energy or am I still in the process of clearing?
_____
_____
_____
_____

❷

I am/was sad about_____
_____
_____

How can I be tender to myself in this situation_____
_____
_____
_____
_____

Where in my body do I feel sadness?_____
_____
_____

Is there a feeling, besides sadness that I am afraid to feel?
_____
_____
_____
_____

Would it feel good to reach out for support? If so, to who?

_____
_____
_____
_____

Is it time to shift my energy or am I still in the process of clearing?

_____
_____
_____
_____

❸

I am/was sad about _____
_____
_____

How can I be tender to myself in this situation _____
_____
_____
_____
_____

Where in my body do I feel sadness? _____
_____
_____

Would it feel good to reach out for support? If so, to who?
___
___
___
___

Is it time to shift my energy or am I still in the process of clearing?
___
___
___
___

I'm Coming HOME TO my BODy's WISDOM

CHAPTER FOUR

CONNECT WITH YOUR INNER CHILD

✡   ✡   ✡

You have an inner child, the emotional, innocent, little you, who prefers to feel rather than think. The problem is it is locked deep within you with its curiosity and creativity but can also be a home for repressed trauma and abuse that you may carry into adulthood.

This chapter aims to help you become an *integrated adult* accountable for your emotional reality and the ability to consider someone's emotional reality too. To become an *integrated adult*, you must do the inner child work, which entails creating a direct line of communication between the little you with all its repressed emotions and the adult you so you can ultimately embody and manifest wisdom and emotional maturity.

Awakening your inner child will allow you to be more joyous daily, have an open mind and total self-expression and embrace your dreams and desires. You must acknowledge your inner child with all its hurts, wants and traumas but not let it drive your life. This allows you to show up in relationships with your more authentic self because if you fail to acknowledge your inner child, it may drive your life without consciousness of the fact on your part.

SELF-REFLECTION AND EXERCISES

Signs of a wounded inner child include fear of abandoment and loss of love, feelings of insecurity, loss your authentic self in a bid to gain the approval of others, seeking instant gratification from substances or distractions, and fear of saying "no" or setting boundaries. Do you relate with any of these? How so?

_____
_____
_____
_____
_____
_____
_____
_____
_____
_____
_____
_____
_____
_____

A wounded inner child in a relationship struggles to understand emotions and express them, it expects their partner to know what they want without vocalizing it, gives the silent treatment when hurt without speaking up; yells and throws tantrums when upset. Do you identify with any of these signs of a wounded inner child? The first step to healing is acceptance. Acknoledge these with specific instances, and promise yourself to work on them.

_____
_____
_____
_____
_____
_____
_____
_____
_____
_____
_____
_____
_____
_____
_____
_____
_____
_____
_____
_____

The next set of questions will help you reflect on your childhood and connect to your inner child better to ease the healing work you will do.

Do you remember your childhood? What was it like growing up?

_____
_____
_____
_____
_____
_____
_____
_____
_____
_____
_____
_____

Were your parents emotionally available or distant?

_____
_____
_____
_____
_____

Were your big emotions validated and held or punished and shamed?

What was the emotional climate in your household growing up - was there joy, celebration and am open conversation about feelings? Or there was gloom and sadness and secrets?

Did you feel celebrated or critisized?

Note: Take time to practice the inner child rituals provided by Sheleana at the end of this chapter.

I CONNECT WITH MY INNER CHILD

PART TWO

HEAL YOUR PAST

"Remember who you are and come home."

CHAPTER FIVE

HEALING THE ABANDONMENT WOUND

✡ ✡ ✡

Underlying almost all human relationships is a desire to feel wanted, loved, cherished, and understood. This desire is amplified for people with a history of abandonment and neglect, which creates what is called the abandonment wound. An abandonment wound is not entirely a mental construct but gets woven into our nervous system, responsible for adaptation and survival. Instead, an abandonment wound causes the nervous system to form maladaptive responses like uncontrolled anger, passive aggression, avoidance, and withdrawal. These maladaptive responses created by an abandonment wound limit us from creating healthy relationships with others.

Abandonment wounds generally form from having physically or emotionally absent parents, betrayal, the death of a friend, or even health complications. And when these wounds are activated, we find ourselves pleasing people to keep love, controlling other people, feeling anxious about being left, and feeling insecure and full of self-doubt.

Healing the abandonment wound means accepting the full spectrum of who you are and being at home with yourself. By so doing, ye create an opening for the right people to enter your life and love you fully. Healing doesn't come from forgetting your wounds or letting them go; rather, it is being with and accepting them as the fullest expression of who you are. Sheleana recommends some practices to help you heal your abandonment wounds. They are; rebuilding a connection with your inner child, letting yourself feel, maintaining boundaries, asking for help, letting love in, and staying committed to your interests, hobbies, and values.

SELF-REFLECTION AND EXERCISES

Do you think you have any abandonment wounds, talk about what you think they might be.

_____
_____
_____
_____
_____
_____
_____
_____
_____
_____
_____
_____
_____
_____
_____
_____
_____
_____
_____
_____
_____
_____
_____
_____

"Healing doesn't come from forgetting your wounds or letting them go; rather, it is being with and accepting them as the fullest expression of who you are." Can you come face to face with, and "live with" your wounds, especially the ones that hurt the most?

Sheleana describes the three abandonment archetypes as "the love chaser," "the ultra-independent," and "over-giver." Which of them are you and why?

Healing means staying committed to your interests hobbies and values in a relationship. Do you do too much to please your partners -like scrapping your plans at the last minute just because they called or working based on their schedule? Highlight specific instances and resolve to remain commited to yourself.

___
___
___
___
___
___
___
___
___
___
___
___
___
___
___
___
___
___
___
___

I HEAL MY WOUNDS

CHAPTER SIX

DIVINE MOTHER AND FATHER ENERGY

✡ ✡ ✡

Our relationship with our parents (father and mother) plays a significant role in shaping the relationships we experience throughout our lives. While you may not have had the opportunity to have deep transformative conversations with your biological parents, doing the inner work of father and mother taught in this chapter will help you connect to the universal divine energy of father and mother and will also help you understand your parents and come to terms with whatever your experience with them was.

Indeed, the very first relationship we have in life is with our parents, who teach us all about love, connection, and safety in the formative years of our lives. The *father-mother wound* thus manifests as the missing sense of protection, love, and acceptance we never received in childhood from our parents. Experiences that may lead to a father-mother wound include growing up in environments where parents fought, emotional or physical abuse was rife, or emotionally shutdown parents who punished you for expressing big emotions like anger, jealousy, or sadness. A father-mother wound often rears its head in a relationship in the form of low self-esteem, codependence, jealousy, self-sabotage, and addiction to chaos and turbulence.

Sheleana shares that a major way to heal your *father-mother wound* is through self-awareness, seeing how you mirror some of your parents' behaviors and patterns, especially if you had a rough time growing up. Recognizing how you are like your parents is an opportunity to deepen self-acceptance and love. By releasing your parents from their roles, you accept that they are only human and reclaim your healing instincts.

Finally, you can cultivate divine mother and father energy by communicating with your inner child, discerning your energy, being the authority of your life, and prioritizing your play and laughter.

SELF-REFLECTION AND EXERCISES

Describe what you remember about your relationship with your parents. What feelings/moments stand out for you?

_____
_____
_____
_____
_____
_____
_____
_____
_____
_____
_____
_____
_____
_____
_____
_____
_____
_____
_____
_____
_____
_____
_____
_____

Sheleana presents eight wounded father-mother archetypes that most of us experienced, including you. Which do you feel you experienced -can you recall specific instances? Note that the point of this exercise is not to criticize or blame your parents. It is simply to help you understand what you were taught about love, bringing into awareness your inherited patterns and ultimately help you release your resentments and put the circle to rest.

_____
_____
_____
_____
_____
_____
_____
_____
_____
_____
_____
_____
_____
_____
_____
_____
_____
_____

Becoming aware of your parents' traits, characteristics, and patterns is the first step to realizing how your relationship with your parents manifest in your present day. The next journaling prompts will help you become aware of those traits. Be advised that the traits you dislike or reject in your parents may also be the traits you struggle to accept in yourself. By leaning into the wounds your parents caused you, you make room for your own integration, and focus on being yourself.

MOTHER

Something I like in my mother is:

___

Qualities of my mother that I reject in myself are:

___

Something I always wanted from my mother is:

___

Qualities of my mother that I like in myself are:

___

FATHER

Something I like in my father is:

___

Qualities of my father that I reject in myself are:

___

Something I always wanted from my father is:

_____
_____
_____
_____
_____

Qualities of my father that I like in myself are:

_____
_____
_____

Take notice of the things you said you always wanted from your father and mother but never received. Do you see any remnants of those longings in your relationships?

_____
_____
_____
_____
_____
_____
_____
_____
_____
_____

Do you think you consistently choose partners who activate that old familiar feeling within you? And is it possible that the love you want is right before you but you cannot see it through your current lens?

MY LETTER RITUAL

Use the space below and on the next pages to write a heartfelt letter to your parent. Tell them all the hurt they caused you, everything you wished you could say to them, what you love and hate about them, all the ways they let you down, what you wish they did differently, everything! The deeper you go, the more you will get out of the process. However, note that this letter is for you, do not send it to your parent under any circumstance..

_____
_____
_____
_____
_____
_____
_____
_____
_____
_____
_____
_____
_____
_____
_____
_____
_____

NOTE: BURNING RITUAL

Tear out the pages of this workbook on which you wrote the letter and keep it on your alter. Whenever you feel ready, burn the pages and pour the ashes in water to dissolve.

I HARNESS DIVINE MOTHER & FATHER ENERGY

CHAPTER SEVEN

FORGIVENESS AND ACCEPTANCE

✡ ✡ ✡

Forgiveness is a word pregnant with meaning for each of us depending on our circumstances, experiences, and the people we spend time with. It is not about finding justifications or excuses for the conduct of others who once hurt or still hurt us; rather, forgiveness provides a deeper context to see the innocence below our layers of hurt, offering us a pathway to set our hearts free from the anger, bitterness, and resentment that comes with unforgiveness.

If you are not careful, feelings of betrayal and hurt can hijack your daily existence and hold you in a circle of never-ending bitterness and internal chaos. You may want those who hurt you to take responsibility and acknowledge the pain they caused you, but you must realize that holding grudges comes at a very high cost for you. Unhealed and unresolved relationships with your parents, siblings, and past partners stay below the surface and wreak havoc in your inner emotional world. Thus, as long as you hold on to resentment and replay past events in your mind, you are never free.

Some acts or inactions are indeed impossible to forgive. All you need do is accept them. Acceptance is the willingness to acknowledge the past for what it is, coupled with the knowledge that you can't change the way things are. Acceptance will help you remove any resentment you may feel that tends to hurt you. However, forgiveness and acceptance do not mean you allow people that hurt you back into your life or that you minimize that hurt you felt. It means accepting that what happened cannot be changed, that you are ready to release yourself from playing the event in your mind repeatedly. Finally, forgiveness and acceptance mean that you no longer want to give anyone power over you by holding on to the anger and fear in your body.

SELF-REFLECTION AND EXERCISES

Forgiveness and acceptance mean that you are ready to release yourself and take back the power anyone holds over you when you hold on to the anger and fear in your body. With this in mind, list out up to five persons you still harbor resentment, anger and any kind of unresolved feelings against. This list should include people who hurt you that you are still carrying in your mind and heart.

❶
_____
_____

❷
_____
_____

❸
_____
_____

❹
_____
_____

❺
_____
_____

THE FORGIVENESS RITUAL (1)

This ritual is a great way to support your forgiveness process. Go back to the list of persons you wrote in the previous page and choose one person to focus on. Write a letter to them saying everything you want to say to them. Don't hold back, tell them how they hurt you, and get as real as you possibly can even if the letter is rageful. Write all that you ever wanted to say to them and all the ways that they let you down. Check out the prompts provided by Sheleana and try expanding on them.

THE FORGIVENESS RITUAL (2)

Pick another person from the previous list and write them a letter following the instructions provided in the previous ritual.

i FORGIVE AND LET GO

PART THREE

EXPLORE YOUR RELATIONSHIP PATTERNS

Release romantic partners from your roles and labels and give room for mystery

CHAPTER EIGHT

UNDERSTANDING PROJECTIONS

✡   ✡   ✡

Learning to trust when we have been hurt is not easy. It's normal and a natural instinct to self-protect when we have a history of being betrayed, hurt or let down. However, the problem is these hurts from the past often show up as projections (a *projection means automatically attributing qualities in us or from someone in the past to some other thing or person in our present*) on the current people in our lives; thereby preventing them from loving us fully because we were hurt in the past. You can't be receptive to love when you're stuck in your projections. The answer lies not in setting rigid boundaries; we can't escape pain by avoiding it. It is about sitting with the pain with all its intensity and relearning what it means to love again.

The first step to healing your projections is to grow and expand your capacity to be with your discomforts when they arise. You can do this by giving yourself a brief moment of pause to enable you to develop the self-awareness with which you realize that you are projecting a past hurt into the present. You must work to increase your awareness in moments greatly charged with emotion because underneath your projections is a vulnerability you need to tend to daily. Ways of managing your vulnerabilities may be through actions like speaking loving words to yourself or even having a good cry.

Finally, the best way to heal your habit of projecting heavily in your relationships is to identify when you are caught in the circle of projections and consequently move out of them. The self-reflection and exercises on the next page will help you with this process.

SELF-REFLECTION AND EXERCISES

Projections take the form of assuming your current partner will behave like the last one, having a strong negative reaction to what someone does because it reminds you of a painful past, unconsciously punishing a present partner for what happened in the past, etc. In what ways do you think you have been projecting in your relationships?

_____
_____
_____
_____
_____
_____
_____
_____
_____
_____
_____
_____
_____
_____
_____
_____
_____
_____

The first step to healing your projections is growing your capacity to be with your disomfort when it arises. The next journal prompts will help you increase your awareness in moments of great emotional intensity. You don't have to fill out the prompts now, wait until one of those times when you feel emotionally tense. The prompts are duplicated so you can use it more than once.

SELF-CENTERING EXERCISE

When you're in conflict, take a breath, cease what you are doing and answer the following prompts:

❶

What am I feeling?

_____
_____
_____
_____
_____

What does this bring up for me?

_____
_____
_____
_____
_____

Who or what does this person remind me of?
_____
_____
_____

What feelings am I pushing away rigt now?
_____
_____
_____
_____
_____

What do I really need that I'm afraid to ask for or don't believe I can have?
_____
_____
_____
_____
_____

What am I afraid to say or feel?
_____
_____
_____
_____
_____

❷

What am I feeling?

_____
_____
_____
_____
_____

What does this bring up for me?

_____
_____
_____
_____
_____

Who or what does this person remind me of?

_____
_____
_____

What feelings am I pushing away rigt now?

_____
_____
_____
_____

What do I really need that I'm afraid to ask for or don't believe I can have?

_____
_____
_____
_____
_____

What am I afraid to say or feel?

_____
_____
_____
_____
_____

"Much of the chaos and heartache we have felt in our relationships is the result of unprocessed pain from our previous history." Do you identify and agree with this statement on some level? How so?

I FREE MY PARTNERS FROM MY PROJECTIONS

CHAPTER NINE

TRANSFORM YOUR RELATIONSHIP PATTERNS

✡ ✡ ✡

Everything is energy, and in this chapter, you will learn how to consciously direct your energy when you see specific patterns toward a place where your life is more enhanced and harmonious. In relationships, a pattern may be seen as recurrent frustrating experiences that occur over several of your relationships, both from the past and present. Such relationship patterns may include running or getting distant at the first sign of conflict, repetitive cheating or being cheated on, chasing unavailable or emotionally unsafe people, instigating conflict and chaos, holding back true expression in a relationship, losing touch of self and your identity in a relationship as well as fearing deep intimacy.

When you start healing your relationship patterns, you unlearn how you have come to defend your heart throughout your lifetime. However, you must realize that your relationship patterns are your work to undertake in a lifetime. They may never fully go away, but their intensity and how they show up will shift and soften as you begin the healing work.

The next section contains questions and exercises to help heal your relationship patterns.

SELF-REFLECTION AND EXERCISES

Sheleana opines that each one of us may have negative relationship patterns that linger over our relationships - like closing ourselves to love, losing ourselves in the other partner etc. What are the patterns you have noticed in your relationships? How do you see yourself in your relationships, is there a belief that continues to resurface?

_____
_____
_____
_____
_____
_____
_____
_____
_____
_____
_____
_____

Sheleana highlights three relationship signatures that each of us carry throughout our lives, namely the Ocean type, Mountain type, and Wind type. Which of the signatures do you carry, and what do you think the signature is trying to teach you?

Now think of the patterns you hae admitted to be existent in your relationships, to break this patterns, you have to see how wounds from the past can keep those old stories alive. What feelings do you try to attain -is it Love? Acceptance? Safety, or Validation? What are the parts you are trying to hide? What are your deepest desires? Declare them. Here and now.

_____
_____
_____
_____
_____
_____
_____
_____
_____
_____
_____
_____
_____
_____
_____
_____
_____
_____
_____
_____

I TRANSFORM MY NEGATIVE RELATIONSHIP PATTERNS

CHAPTER TEN

COMPASSIONATE SELF-AWARENESS

✡   ✡   ✡

Many children are parented through the dysfunctional counterproductive method of punishment and shame. However, punishment and humiliation do not teach us to be better people; it leads us to think something about ourselves is not okay, then we tend to self-reject and internalize this sense of rejection we feel. The right way to effect change in a child's life is through emotional connection, encouragement, and praise; hence such change will never come through criticism, judgment, and self-blame.

Punishment and humiliation also lead to self-rejection, and as long as you believe you are broken or not good enough, you cannot heal because at the very root of your patterns is the belief that you deserve suffering.

However, all hope is not lost as you have the power to take over ownership of your life through self-compassion, self-acceptance, and self-forgiveness.

Healing, you must realize, demands true accountability, which must be paired with self-compassion to be effective. Being accountable for your patterns requires that you look inwards to find what you're avoiding in yourself whenever you judge, criticize, or blame others. It is not about blaming yourself; it is rather about harnessing the power to show up more consciously in your relationships. Moreover, the purpose of the accountability work is self-acceptance, which liberates and paves the way for deeper transformation.

SELF-REFLECTION AND EXERCISES

The Acountability Work

This journaling session will help you gain self-acceptance and compassion for yourself by shining a light inward. Answer the prompts below, giving yourself grace and compassion through the process. However, you must note that you cannot heal completely by journaling alone; you don't really have to "do" anything with these journal prompts. They are designed to help you feel more connected to yourself so you can understand what's going on beneath your reactions and defenses, consequently helping you have deeper compassion for yourself.

What is your default emotion in conflict? Do you feel fear, anger, sadness, anxiety, or something different?

___

What emotion are you the most afraid of in others?

___

What judgements do you have about that emotion that you hate in others?

_____
_____
_____
_____

Do you let yourself express or feel that emotion? When you do, what happens?

_____
_____
_____
_____

Are there any recurrent feelings from childhood that tend to pop up in your adult relationships (e.g., feeling unheard, abandoned etc)?

_____
_____
_____
_____
_____
_____

How do you tend to express yourself when you are upset? Is it by yelling, crying, attacking, blaming, shutting down? etc.

What traits or characteristics repulse you the most in other people (e.g., jealousy, anger, envy, greed etc)?

Do you see those characteristics you don't like in others in yourself? How does it show up? Dive deep, be truthful and honest to yourself here.

What side of yourself automatically shows up when you're most comfortable with someone or your closest friends (e.g., silly, laughter, serious, etc)?

___

What do people assume about you that feels hurtful?

___

What do you wish people saw in you?

___

How could you practice embodying more of what you wish people saw in you?

What emotion would you like to learn how to be more comfortable with?

What is a pattern or habit of behavior you are ready to shift?

I'M NOT PERFECT BUT IT'S OKAY

CHAPTER ELEVEN

RED FLAGS GREEN FLAGS

✡ ✡ ✡

Sheleana explains red flags, green flags, and yellow flags in this chapter. However, the focus is on the green flags because, more often than not, everyone looks out for the red flags and in so doing, only consistently meet people who fit their criteria for the red flags.

The red, yellow, and green flags collectively help break down behavior into categories. Red flags represent unacceptable and dangerous behaviors; yellow flags are a warning to pay attention, while green flags represent a healthy and connected relationship.

Signs of red flags include abusive language when speaking about an ex or a family member, anger or aggression towards strangers, controlling behavior, jealousy and violation of personal space of partners, rude or insensitive sexual behavior, etc. On the other hand, virtually every relationship will have yellow flags; signs of yellow flags include keeping secrets or lying, debt, lack of ability to have vulnerable conversations, canceling at the last minute, etc. Yellow flags are usually a cue to have direct and clear conversations about whether you are ready to make the relationship work.

Finally, green flags represent a go-ahead. Green flags in a relationship mean you feel safe to express yourself openly, disagreements do not threaten the relationship, each person is responsible for their energy, etc.

However, you should focus on the green flags and direct your energy toward cultivating healthy relationships instead of constantly looking out for red flags. Sometimes you might experience what Sheleana calls false alarms, but it would help if you get help from a trusted therapist or guide to help you navigate these situations.

SELF-REFLECTION AND EXERCISES

Take an inward look into yourself. Do you always dwell on the red flags in your relationships? How can you direct your energy towards working for, and seeing the green flags?

Communication is key to creating reality checks which quieten the fears that lead you to assumptions. Do you communicate with your partner or immediately make assumptions? How can you communicate more and assume less?

I BELIEVE IN ME.

PART FOUR

REALIGN WITH YOUR TRUTH

"Sometimes what looks like rejection is actually a calling into power."

CHAPTER TWELVE

TRUST YOUR BODY, SET BOUNDARIES.

✡ ✡ ✡

Boundaries are imaginary lines that demarcate our feelings, needs, responsibilities, and the totality of our Self from other people. Setting proper boundaries enables us to create healthier relationships where we feel seen, respected, and loved for who we truly are. This is because individuals with no proper boundaries tend to be people-pleasers with no sense of identity and self-worth. Thus, when setting boundaries, you must be clear about your intentions by asking yourself whether you are creating such boundaries to invite a person closer or to protect yourself and whether you are creating the boundaries from a place of fear or a place of love for your self.

You must create five types of boundaries: physical, material, emotional, mental, and spiritual. However, it is your responsibility to clearly and directly communicate your boundaries to your partners from the get-go; hence they can't read your mind.

Finally, though it may come across as aggressive when

you first start setting boundaries, keep trying and continue practicing being true to yourself in an authentic way.

The journaling prompts in the exercises on the next page will help you bring your unique understanding of boundaries to the fore so you can trust yourself and ultimately feel confident expressing your needs.

SELF-REFLECTION AND EXERCISES

What is your unique understanding about boundaries and what they are for?

_____
_____
_____
_____
_____
_____
_____
_____
_____
_____
_____
_____
_____
_____
_____
_____
_____
_____
_____
_____
_____
_____
_____

Have you ever created boundaries in your life before this moment? Did you create such boundaries from a place of fear, or from a place of love?

_____
_____
_____
_____
_____
_____
_____
_____
_____
_____
_____
_____
_____
_____
_____
_____
_____
_____
_____
_____
_____
_____

Have you ever mistaken walls for boundaries in your life? How so?

_____
_____
_____
_____
_____
_____
_____
_____
_____

Can you remember times in your life when you felt guilty for setting a boundary?

_____
_____
_____
_____
_____
_____
_____
_____
_____

Do you believe that boundaries make you powerful? If yes, do you feel safe in your power?

_____
_____
_____
_____
_____
_____
_____
_____
_____
_____

Is there any part of you that believes that if you are powerful, you will hurt others?

_____
_____
_____
_____
_____
_____
_____

I SET HEALTHY BOUNDARIES AND I RESPECT THEM

CHAPTER THIRTEEN

CLARIFY YOUR EXPECTATIONS

✡ ✡ ✡

No relationship is perfect. There will always be good and bad days. This reality must sink deep in you because, in the endless quest for a perfect relationship, you may lose sight of the fact that no human is perfect and can give you an endless stream of bliss.

All you need do is have realistic expectations for your relationship because there will still be moments of conflict and misunderstanding. What you should look out for is a partner who is ready to put in the work to make the relationship work. Despite having expectations, you are allowed to want what you want. It is not unrealistic to expect love, safety, trust, and respect from a partner. You deserve all that.

Thus, you can set a foundation for a conscious relationship by realizing which of your expectations are realistic and which are not. The journal prompts in the exercises section will help you with this process.

SELF-REFLECTION AND EXERCISES

Have you ever had any expectations for your relationships before now? Would you now consider any of them as unrealistic?

_____
_____
_____
_____
_____
_____
_____
_____

How can you describe your relationship to conflict in your relationships? What do you notice?

_____
_____
_____
_____
_____
_____
_____
_____

What are some of the biggest dissapointments you have experienced in your relationships?

Tune in now for a moment and reconsider those dissapointments mentioned above. Were they amplified by the belief that things were supposed to happen in a certain way but they didn't?

_____
_____
_____
_____
_____
_____
_____
_____
_____
_____
_____
_____
_____
_____
_____
_____
_____
_____
_____
_____
_____

Creating My Expectations

| Unrealistic Expectations I had | Realistic Expectations I am creating. |

How do you think your relationship should look and be?

I Clarify my EXPECTATIONS

CHAPTER FOURTEEN

DEFINE YOUR CORE VALUES

✡ ✡ ✡

The qualities that are most important to you are your core values. These core values are your life's guiding beliefs and principles. They may include values like respect, integrity, honesty, loyalty, and generosity. Defining your core values is very important because knowing your truth makes it easier to communicate them and will prevent you from adopting the values of those around you because you know what you need to stay aligned. Despite having your core values, you must still leave a little space for people to wiggle in; because rather than scrutinizing the details or mistakes others have made in the past, it's much easier to trust your choices. Moreover, sometimes those with the most past baggage are the readiest to show up and make a relationship work because they have made peace with their demons.

You may also need to reclaim your core values by assessing what beliefs or behaviors you adopted based on your family values ad learning to set aside what doesn't belong to you so you can claim what is truly yours.

Lastly, you have to embody your core values.

If you need commitment from your partners, in what ways are you showing commitment? If you want respect in a relationship, are you respectful? This is a daily practice you must imbibe.

The exercises for this chapter will explore and deepen your relationship with your core values.

SELF-REFLECTION AND EXERCISES

The self-reflection questions contained below will help you define your core values.

What core value(s) did you inherit from your parents that is true for you?

___
___
___
___

What core value(s) have you inherited and are loyal to but is not true to you?

___
___
___
___

Which core values do you prioritize in a relationship?

___
___
___
___

What core values do you tend to neglect in a relationship?

_____
_____
_____
_____
_____

In choosing your past partners, what values do your choices show that you prioritized?

_____
_____
_____
_____
_____

How did those choices impact your relationships?

_____
_____
_____
_____
_____
_____

What core values continue to be important to you?

What core values are you not ready to compromise going forwards?

Embodying My Core Values

In the exercise that follows, highlight your core values on the one hand and how you will embody them on the other.

My Core Values	How I will Embody Them

I DEFINE AND EMBODY MY CORE VALUES

PART FOUR

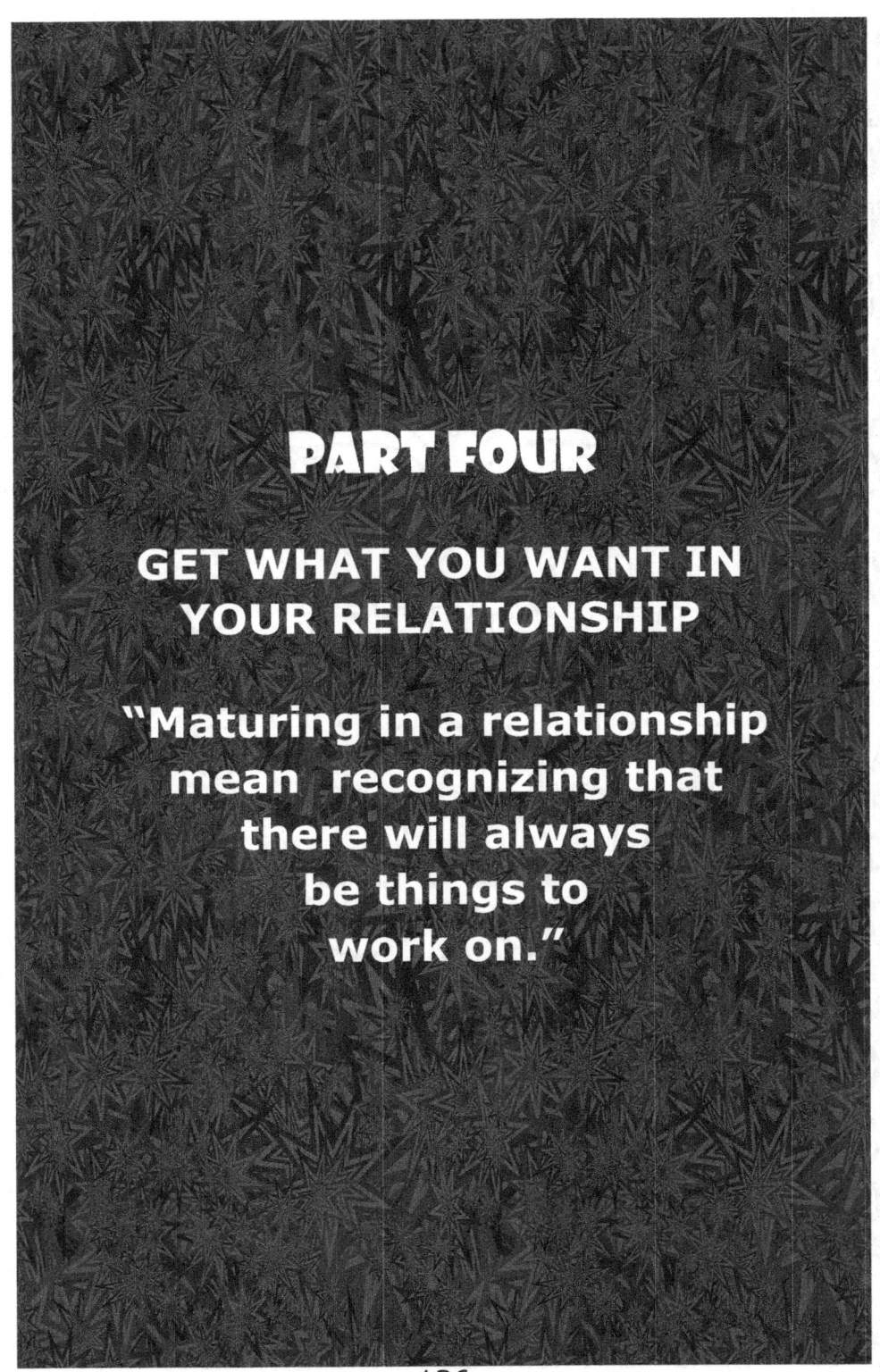

GET WHAT YOU WANT IN YOUR RELATIONSHIP

"Maturing in a relationship mean recognizing that there will always be things to work on."

CHAPTER FIFTEEN

CREATING A CONSCIOUS RELATIONSHIP
✡ ✡ ✡

Relationships are an interesting aspect of life that help us evolve spiritually and otherwise. If we are willing and intentional, relationships help us sit in the fire of self-transformation. Thus, this chapter will help you embrace the beauty that relationships can bring to your life by creating a new lens for how to see relationships and their purpose in your life. This new lens will help you see what a conscious relationship is.

There are two types of relationships; a conventional, non-growth-oriented relationship and a conscious, growth-oriented one. Conscious relationships entail having a clean relationship with yourself and bringing presence, honesty, and an open mind into any relationship. It means being authentic, listening to your body, taking time to get to know your partner on a deeper level, asking important questions and being genuinely curious about your partner, etc.

Lastly, like a planted seed, you must tend to and water

your relationship daily through a daily recommitment to show up with an open heart; be committed to self-awareness; be engaged in healing wounds from the past, and be willing to apologize and practice acceptance and forgiveness.

SELF-REFLECTION AND EXERCISES

Sheleana provides five relationship stages, the *no relationship zone, honeymoon phase, power struggle, twilight zone,* and the *Power Grid* relationship. Which stage do you recognize most in your past relationships and have you ever had any experience of a power grid relationship? If so, what did you and your partner do differently?

_____
_____
_____
_____
_____
_____
_____
_____
_____
_____
_____
_____
_____
_____
_____
_____
_____

Are you in a relationship or currently in the talking stage with anyone? Sheleana recommends that you ask yourself some questions about your partner and answer them truthfully to enable you qualify your relationship. So, provide answers to the questions below with your partner or potential partner in mind.

Do you like how the person speaks to you or others? Why or Why not?

_____
_____
_____
_____

Do you know who the person is, what their past is, and what their core values are when it comes to love and intimacy?

_____
_____
_____
_____
_____
_____
_____

Is the person someone you feel like you could be close friends with, or is it just sexual attraction?

_____
_____
_____
_____
_____
_____

Do you want something from the person that you feel might be coming from an unconscious place?

_____
_____
_____
_____
_____
_____

Do you feel like you want the person to tell you you're good enough, or to validate you in some way?

_____
_____
_____
_____
_____
_____

Do you feel relaxed in your body, and safe to express yourself with the person?

___

Can you have fun, laugh and be playful with the person? Does the connection feel expansive?

___

I CREATE CONSCIOUS RELATIONSHIPS

CHAPTER SIXTEEN

YOUR PATH TO AUTHENTIC LOVE

✡ ✡ ✡

No matter who you are and what you want, when you choose to live in alignment with your dreams and values, you come to realize your worth that is stationed deep within your soul. When you claim your voice, you become unstoppable and inspirational.

When you understand and imbibe authentic love, you no longer breathe by the judgments or expectations of others. You clear the path in your life to be a reflection of the authentic version of yourself rather than your wounds. In this chapter, you will finally create your path to authentic love through the exercises on the next page.

SELF-REFLECTION AND EXERCISES

Your path to authentic love involves creating a conscious love map which is a creative process designed to connect you to heart, your essence, and what you truly want. Answer the questions below and perform the exercise to create your conscious love map.

Step 1: Envisioning the Love You Want

What is your vision of a fulfilling relationship that will give you feelings of contentment, ease, connection, and intimacy?

_____
_____
_____
_____
_____

If you weren't afraid to claim what you truly desire in love, what would you wish for?

_____
_____
_____
_____
_____

What kind of person do you want to attract as a partner? Describe as many traits as comes to mind.

_____
_____
_____
_____
_____
_____
_____
_____
_____
_____

Who do you want to show up as in your relationship? How do you feel, act, and how does your partner experience you?

_____
_____
_____
_____
_____
_____
_____
_____

How do you want to assert your boundaries? (Describe how and when you will communicate your boundaries.

How do you want love? What does loving someone look and feel like for you?

Will you be led by love or fear? What does being led by love look like? And what does being led by fear look like?

What are you willing to do to cocreate a healthy and fulfilling relationship?

How are commited to showing up when things get tough, when conflicts arise, or when old wounds get triggered? (Consider how you will navigate conflict, what steps you'll take and how you will support yourself and your relationsips through the inevitable trials of life).

A Day-in-the-Life of My Dream Future

In this letter to yourself, describe what you want your dream relationship and life to be. Write in the present and be as imaginative as possible. What would a day in the life you desire look like?

MY LOVE MAP

Use this page to draw your love map according to Sheleana's instructions.

What was your experience with Becoming the One? Did it meet your expectations? In what ways did it, and in what ways did it not?

i AM THE ONE

ABOUT EAGLE READS

Do you have so much to do but no time? Busy schedules and deadlines creeping up on you? A thousand and one things to attend to, leaving you no time to read all the books you want to read? Worry no longer!

EAGLE READS is a busy man's solution to the busy person's problem. We are a group of experienced writers committed to providing you detail-oriented, straight-to-the-point, and high quality workbooks for, and summaries of lifechanging books by the world's best authors. We sift through the fluff and help you strike gold with each page you turn so you can become golden in as little time as possible.